Flower Children Quilt

Oxmoor House®

Flower Children Quilt
©2000 by Oxmoor House Inc.
Book Division of Southern Progress Corporation
P.O. Box 2463
Birmingham, Alabama 35201

Published by Oxmoor House, Inc. and Leisure Arts, Inc.

ISBN: 0-8487-2388-0
Printed in the United States of America
First Printing 2000

Editor-in-Chief: Nancy Fitzpatrick Wyatt
Senior Crafts Editor: Susan Ramey Cleveland
Senior Editor, Copy and Homes: Olivia Kindig Wells
Art Director: James Boone

Flower Children Quilt
Editors: Catherine Corbett Fowler, Lois Martin
Copy Editor: L. Amanda Owens
Contributing Copy Editor: Susan Cheatham
Designer and Illustrator: Kelly Davis
Senior Photographer: John O'Hagan
Photo Stylist: Linda Baltzell Wright
Director, Production and Distribution: Phillip Lee
Books Production Manager: Theresa L. Beste
Production Manager, Continuities and Magazines: Greg Amason
Production Assistant: Faye Porter Bonner

We're Here for You!
We at Oxmoor House are dedicated to serving you with reliable information that expands your imagination and enriches your life. We welcome your comments and suggestions.

Please write us at:

Oxmoor House
Editor, Flower Children Quilt
2100 Lakeshore Drive
Birmingham, AL 23209

To order additional publications, call 1-800-633-4910.

Flower Children Quilt designed and made by Carol Burger.

Contents

Welcome!

The happy little blossoms of this whimsical quilt seem to beckon to you to come and spend the day with them. **Just looking at them makes one feel a little lighthearted.**

And best of all, you don't have to spend hours and hours working on this project before you can begin to enjoy it. **Quick techniques, such as fusible appliqué, pen stitching, and tying, mean you can make this quilt in a few days.**

The finished size of the Flower Children Quilt is only 35" x 43$\frac{1}{2}$", just right to decorate a nook or a cranny in your home. **If you prefer a larger quilt, you can enlarge the patterns accordingly.** For instance, if you want to make the blocks 12" instead of 7", use a photocopier to enlarge the appliqué patterns to 174% of their original size. Then cut your background squares 12$\frac{1}{2}$" and cut sashing and borders to fit.

These versatile appliqué designs can also be applied to a variety of projects. Use them to embellish a purchased shirt, tote bag, or garden apron. Fuse them to kitchen towels, place mats, T-shirts, or garden gloves to make adorable gifts for all your friends and family.

Just use your own imagination along with the patterns and the instructions in this book to plant your own spring garden of flower children.

General Instructions

Please read instructions before cutting appliqué pieces. Instructions given are for fused appliqué. Appliqué patterns do not include seam allowances. For machine appliqué, cut pieces finished size (without seam allowances); for hand appliqué, add 1/8" seam allowances.

We based fabric requirements on 44"-wide fabric with trimmed selvages and made generous allowances to account for shrinkage and individual differences in cutting. Wash, dry, and press fabrics before cutting.

See "Tips and Tidbits" (page 26) before beginning your quilt.

Finished Size: 35" x 43 1/2"

Blocks: 12 (7") squares

Materials

1 3/8 yards beige print for blocks and borders
1 yard green print for sashing and binding
1/4 yard white for picket fences and bumblebee wings
1/8 yard light yellow for flower faces
Assorted scraps in various shades of red, yellow, green, blue, and brown for block and border appliqués
1 3/8 yards fabric for backing
1 1/2 yards paper-backed fusible web
Plastic or cardboard for templates (optional for machine or hand appliqué)
1/4 yard 1/8"-wide red ribbon
Assorted charms and buttons, assorted colors of embroidery floss, assorted colors of thread, and thin twine for embellishments

Background Squares and Border Cutting

From beige print, cut:

- 12 (7 1/2") background squares
- 2 (4 1/2" x 36") side borders
- 2 (4 1/2" x 35 1/2") top and bottom borders

From green print, cut:

- 8 (2" x 7 1/2") vertical sashing strips
- 5 (2" x 24 1/2") horizontal sashing strips
- 2 (2" x 36") outside vertical sashing strips
- 12"-wide crosswise strip for binding

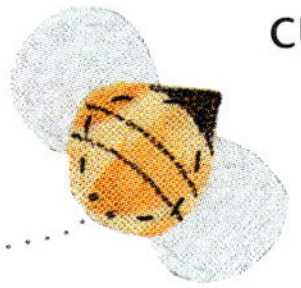

Appliqué Cutting

For block appliqués

Referring to "Applying Fusible Web" below and appliqué cutting lists on pages 7–18, cut out pieces for blocks as needed from fabric scraps. Refer to photos for colors or cut as desired. Cut one of each piece unless otherwise indicated.

For border appliqués

From scraps, cut:

- Pattern 2, bumblebee wings (Cut 7.)
- Pattern 3, bumblebee body (Cut 7.)
- Pattern 7, leaf (Cut 32.)
- Pattern 19, baby flower face (Cut 8.)*
- Pattern 32, large flower center (Cut 8.)*
- Pattern 59, border flower (Cut 12.)
- Pattern 60, flower center (Cut 12.)
- Pattern 61, border flower (Cut 7.)
- Pattern 62, flower center (Cut 7.)
- Pattern 63, border tulip (Cut 12.)

*Use Pattern 32 as flower and Pattern 19 as flower center

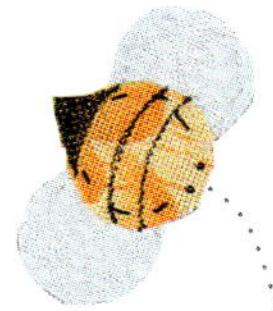

From white, cut:

- Pattern 64, border fence post (Cut 15.)
- 2 (1/2" x 17") strips for fence rails on sides of quilt
- 1/2" x 16" strip for fence rail on bottom of quilt

Embellishment: 1 ladybug-shaped button

Applying Fusible Web

Note: Patterns are reversed for fusible appliqué.

1. For each, trace pattern onto paper (smooth) side of fusible web. (Adhesive side has rougher texture.) Leaving about 1/4" margin around shape, use paper scissors to cut out design.

2. Place adhesive (rough) side of web on wrong side of appliqué fabric. Following manufacturer's instructions, fuse web to fabric. Do not overheat. If desired, use a dry press cloth between iron and adhesive to avoid getting adhesive on iron.

3. Let fabric cool completely. Then use fabric scissors to cut out design along drawn line.

4. To mark detail or embroidery lines, place cutout over reversed pattern or over block photo and, using pencil, lightly trace lines onto right side of fabric shape.

Fusing Instructions

1. Peel off paper backing from appliqué pieces.
2. With web side down, position appliqué on right side of background material. When sure of placement, cover appliqué with a damp press cloth. Fuse in place, following manufacturer's instructions. (Heavy fabrics may require more pressing time.) Remove press cloth and iron project to eliminate excess moisture. Let fabric cool.
3. Where appliqués overlap, start fusing pieces in back of design (underneath pieces) and work up to front (topmost) pieces. If one piece is layered atop another, cut out base shape but do not peel away protective paper. Lightly fuse second piece in place on base. Peel paper off base piece and use full heat to fuse combined appliqué in place.

Block Assembly

Refer to block photos to fuse pieces in place and to add embellishments and pen stitching as desired.

Quilt Top Assembly

1. Referring to Quilt Top Assembly Diagram, join 3 blocks and 2 (7½") vertical sashing strips as shown to make 1 horizontal row. Repeat to make 3 more rows.
2. Join block rows with 1 (24½") horizontal sashing strip between each row. Join remaining sashing strips to top and bottom.
3. Join 36" outside vertical sashing strips to sides.
4. For outer border, join 36" beige print strips to sides. Then join 35½" beige print strips to top and bottom.
5. Referring to photo on page 4, fuse border appliqué designs in place.

Quilting and Finishing

1. Layer backing (facedown), batting, and quilt top (faceup). Baste. Quilt or tie as desired. Quilt shown is tied at corners of each block, using 1 strand of thin twine. Be sure to stitch through all 3 layers to secure. Tie tails in tight bows.
2. Make approximately 170" of straight-grain binding from green print. Add to quilt.

Quilt Top Assembly Diagram

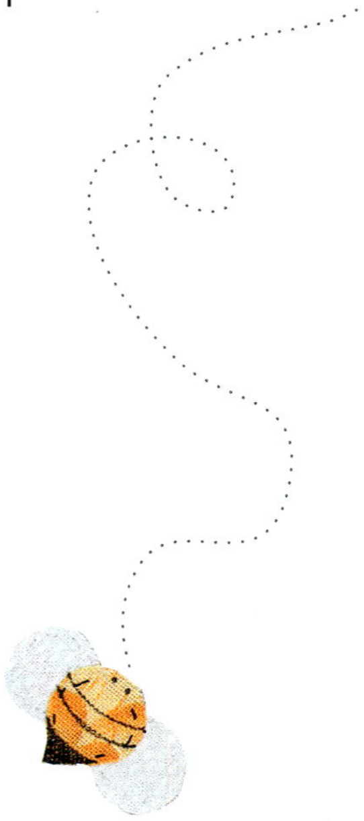

Block Cutting Instructions

Good Morning, Sunshine

From scraps, cut:

- Pattern 2, bumblebee wings
- Pattern 3, bumblebee body
- Pattern 4, sun center
- Pattern 5, sunrays
- Pattern 6, sunray (Cut 4.)
- Pattern 7, leaf (Cut 2.)
- Pattern 8, petal (Cut 7.)
- 1/4" x 1 1/4" strip for stem

From light yellow, cut:

- Pattern 1, small flower face

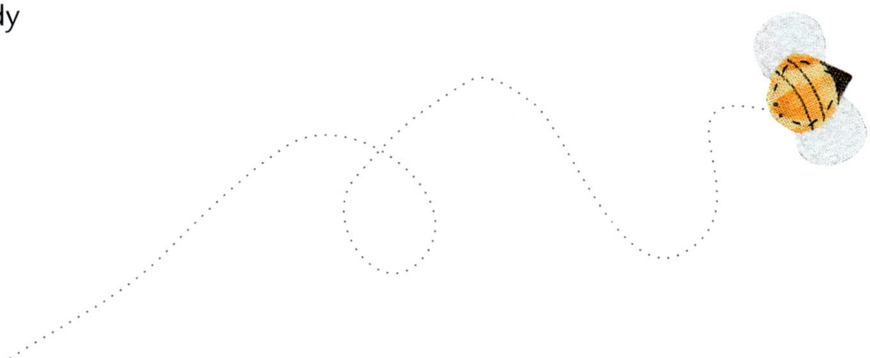

Jump Rope Jenny

From scraps, cut:
- Pattern 2, bumblebee wings (Cut 2.)
- Pattern 3, bumblebee body (Cut 2.)
- Pattern 9, dress
- Pattern 10 and 10 reversed, leaf
- Pattern 11, petal (Cut 5.)

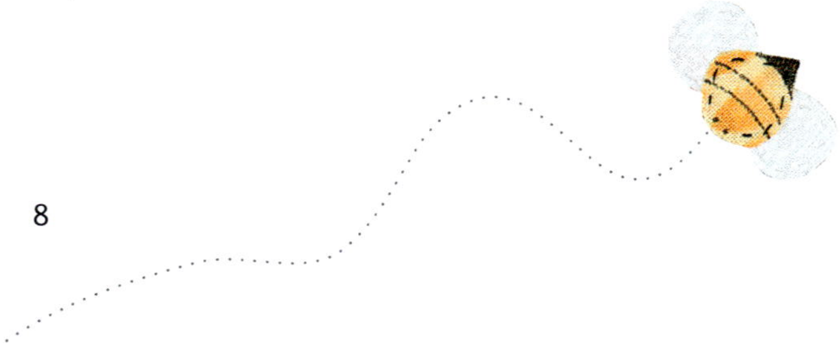

From light yellow, cut:
- Pattern 1, small flower face

Embellishments: 8" length 1/8"-wide red satin ribbon, 3 (3/8") red heart-shaped buttons, 2 (1/4") white buttons
(See "Tips and Tidbits" on page 26 for adding the ribbon embellishment *before* fusing the bumblebees.)

Daisy Darlin'

From scraps, cut:

- Pattern 2, bumblebee wings
- Pattern 3, bumblebee body
- Pattern 12, dress
- Pattern 12A, back of dress (Cut from wrong side of fabric.)
- Pattern 13 and 13 reversed, sleeve
- Pattern 13A and 13A reversed, back of sleeve (Cut from wrong side of fabric.)
- Pattern 14 and 14 reversed, collar
- Pattern 15, daisy petal (Cut 9.)
- ¼" x 1¼" strip for stem
- 2 (¼" x ¾") strips for arms

From light yellow, cut:

- Pattern 1, small flower face

Embellishment: 1 (½") dark yellow flower-shaped button

Suzie Seedpack

From scraps, cut:
- Pattern 2, bumblebee wings
- Pattern 3, bumblebee body
- Pattern 12, dress
- Pattern 12A, back of dress (Cut from wrong side of fabric.)
- Pattern 13 and 13 reversed, sleeve
- Pattern 13A and 13A reversed, back of sleeve (Cut from wrong side of fabric.)
- Pattern 16, flower petals
- Pattern 17, seed packet
- Pattern 18, leaf (Cut 5.)
- ¼" x 1⅜" strip for stem
- ¼" x ½" strip for neck
- ⅛" x 1¼" strip for arm

From light yellow, cut:
- Pattern 1, small flower face

Embellishments: charms, twine

Basket of Babes

From scraps, cut:

- Pattern 2, bumblebee wings (Cut 2.)
- Pattern 3, bumblebee body (Cut 2.)
- Pattern 20, baby petals
- Pattern 21, baby petals
- Pattern 22, baby petals
- Pattern 23, basket
- Pattern 24, basket handle (Or cut ¼" x 6¾" bias strip.)
- Pattern 25 and 25 reversed, leaf (Cut 8 of #25; cut 5 of #25 reversed.)

From light yellow, cut:

- Pattern 19, baby flower face (Cut 3.)

Sun Hat Sally

From scraps, cut:

- Pattern 2, bumblebee wings
- Pattern 3, bumblebee body
- Pattern 12 reversed, dress
- Pattern 12A reversed, back of dress (Cut from wrong side of fabric.)
- Pattern 18, leaf (Cut 4.)
- Pattern 26, hat
- Pattern 27, flower petals
- Pattern 28, bow (Cut 2.)
- Pattern 29 and 29 reversed, ribbon
- Pattern 30 and 30 reversed, sleeve
- Pattern 31, collar
- 1⁄4" x 1 1⁄4" strip for stem

From light yellow, cut:

- Pattern 1, small flower face

Embellishments: charm, floss

Sunflower Sisters

From scraps, cut:
- Pattern 2, bumblebee wings
- Pattern 3, bumblebee body
- Pattern 18, leaf (Cut 4.)
- Pattern 33, flower petals
- Pattern 34, flower petals
- ¼" x 4¼" strip for long stem
- ¼" x 3" strip for short stem

From light yellow, cut:
- Pattern 1, small flower center
- Pattern 32, large flower center

Picket Fence Posies

From scraps, cut:

- Pattern 2, bumblebee wings
- Pattern 3, bumblebee body
- Pattern 36 and 36 reversed, leaf (Cut 3 of each.)
- Pattern 37, leaf (Cut 7.)

From white, cut:

- Pattern 35, fence post (Cut 5.)
- 2 (½" x 7½") strips for fence rails

Embellishments: 6 (½") flower-shaped buttons in assorted colors, 1 (½") ladybug-shaped button, floss

Clay Pot Cuties

From scraps, cut:

- Pattern 2, bumblebee wings (Cut 2.)
- Pattern 3, bumblebee body (Cut 2.)
- Pattern 38, heart
- Pattern 39, flower face (Cut 2.)
- Pattern 40 and 40 reversed, petal (Cut 2 of each.)
- Pattern 41 and 41 reversed, leaf (Cut 2 of each.)
- Pattern 42, flowerpot rim
- Pattern 43, flowerpot
- 2 ($\frac{1}{4}$" x $1\frac{1}{2}$") strips for stems

Embellishments: charms, floss

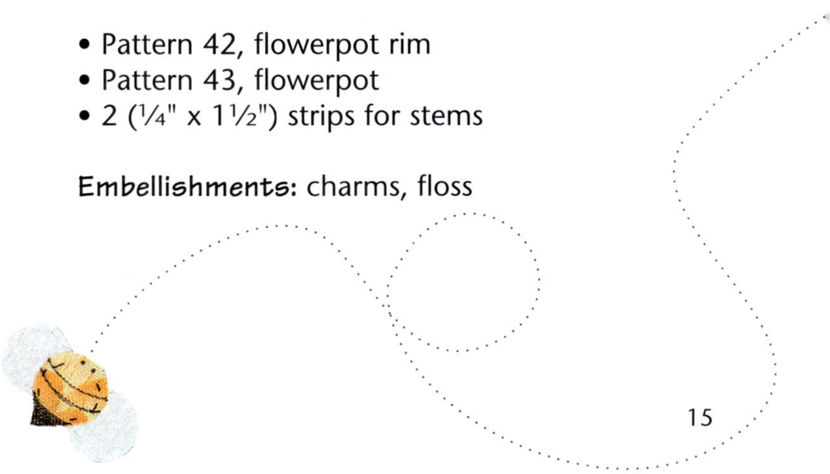

Bucket Buddies

From scraps, cut:
- Pattern 2, bumblebee wings (Cut 2.)
- Pattern 3, bumblebee body (Cut 2.)
- Pattern 18, leaf (Cut 3.)
- Pattern 44, flower petals
- Pattern 45, flower petals
- Pattern 46, flower petals
- Pattern 47, bird body
- Pattern 48, wing
- Pattern 49, beak
- Pattern 50, shoe (Cut 2.)
- Pattern 50A, inside of shoe (Cut 2.)
- Pattern 51, bucket
- Pattern 52, handle
- Pattern 53, water puddle

From light yellow, cut:
- Pattern 1, small flower face (Cut 3.)

Embellishments: 2 (3/8") buttons, floss

Black-eyed Susan

From scraps, cut:

- Pattern 2, bumblebee wings
- Pattern 3, bumblebee body
- Pattern 12, dress
- Pattern 12A, back of dress (Cut from wrong side of fabric.)
- Pattern 13 and 13 reversed, sleeve
- Pattern 13A and 13A reversed, back of sleeve (Cut from wrong side of fabric.)
- Pattern 54, flower petals
- Pattern 55, pocket (Cut 2.)
- 1⁄4" x 1⁄2" strip for neck
- 1⁄4" x 1 1⁄4" strip for stem
- 2 (1⁄4" x 1 1⁄2") strips for arms

From light yellow, cut:

- Pattern 1, small flower face

Peekaboo Tulips

From scraps, cut:

- Pattern 2, bumblebee wings
- Pattern 3, bumblebee body
- Pattern 56 and 56 reversed, leaf (Cut 4 of each.)
- Pattern 57, tulip petals (Cut 4.)
- Pattern 58, tulip face (Cut 4.)
- 2 ($\frac{1}{4}$" x 1$\frac{1}{2}$") strips for stems

Embellishment: 1 heart-shaped button (Or use Pattern 38, heart.)

Patterns

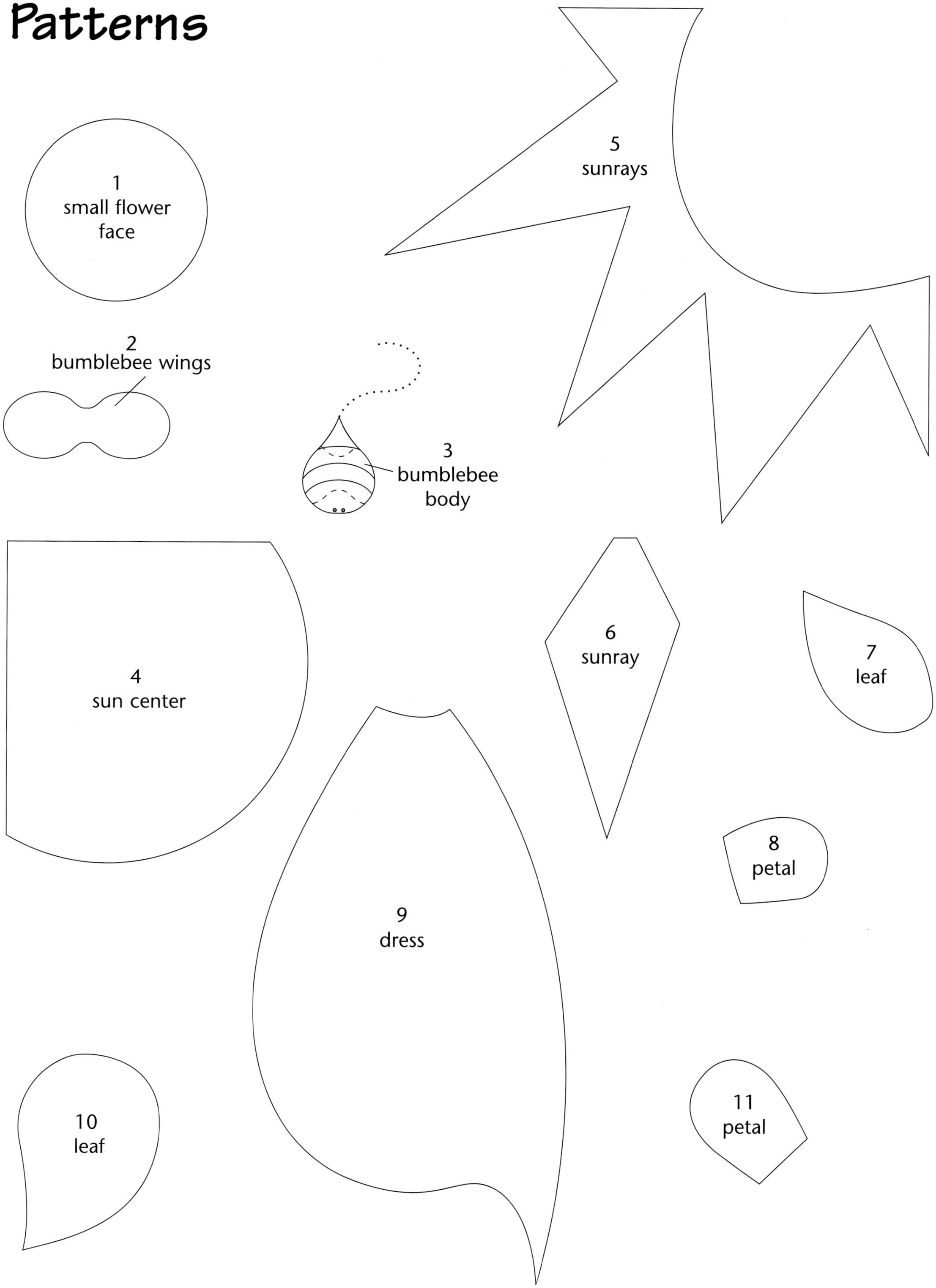
1
small flower face
2
bumblebee wings
3
bumblebee body
4
sun center
5
sunrays
6
sunray
7
leaf
8
petal
9
dress
10
leaf
11
petal

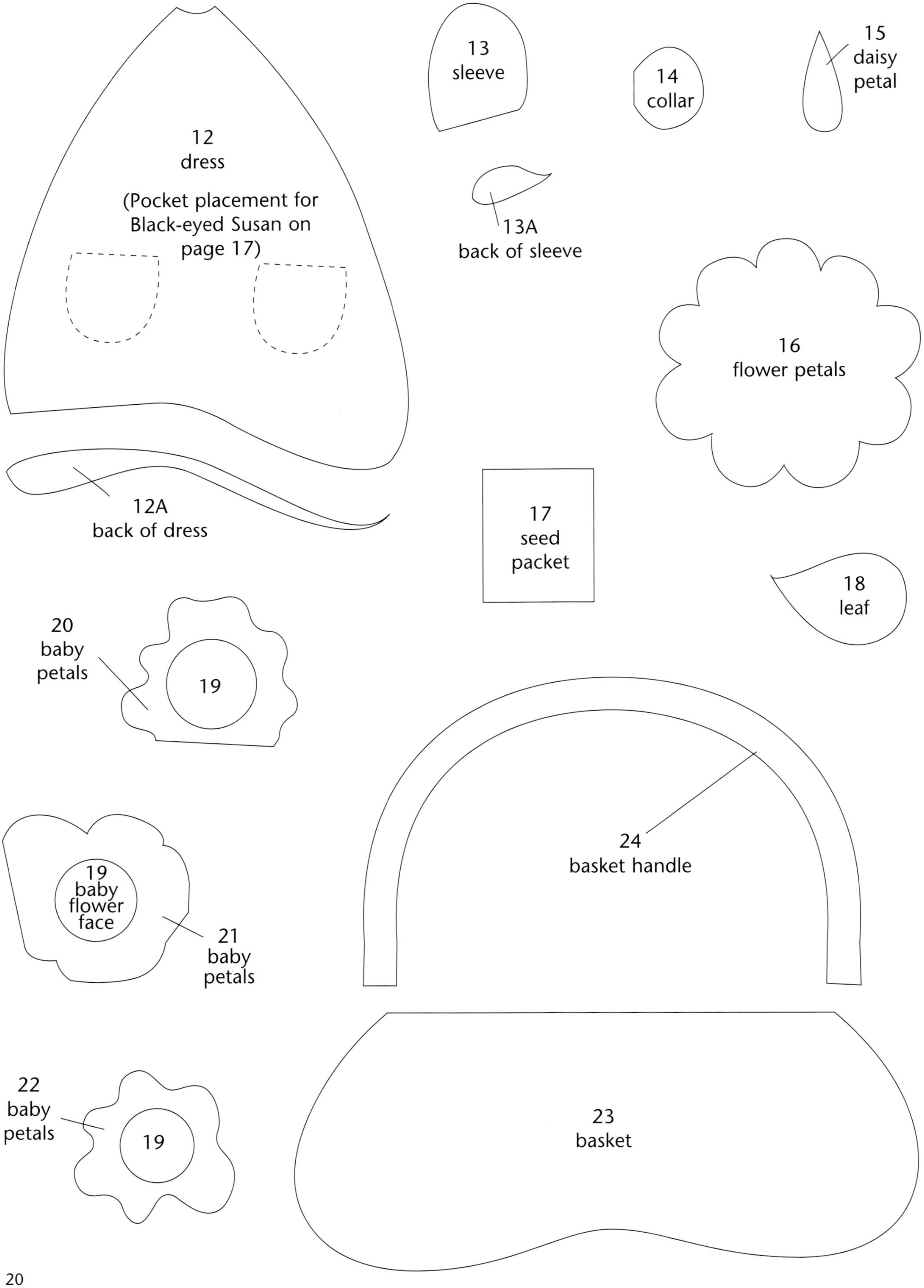
12
dress
(Pocket placement for Black-eyed Susan on page 17)
12A
back of dress
13
sleeve
13A
back of sleeve
14
collar
15
daisy
petal
16
flower petals
17
seed
packet
18
leaf
20
baby
petals
19
19
baby
flower
face
21
baby
petals
22
baby
petals
19
24
basket handle
23
basket

25 leaf
26 hat
27 flower petals
28 bow
29 ribbon
30 sleeve
31 collar
32 large flower center
33 flower petals
34 flower petals
35 fence post
36 leaf
37 leaf
38 heart
39 flower face
40 petal
41 leaf

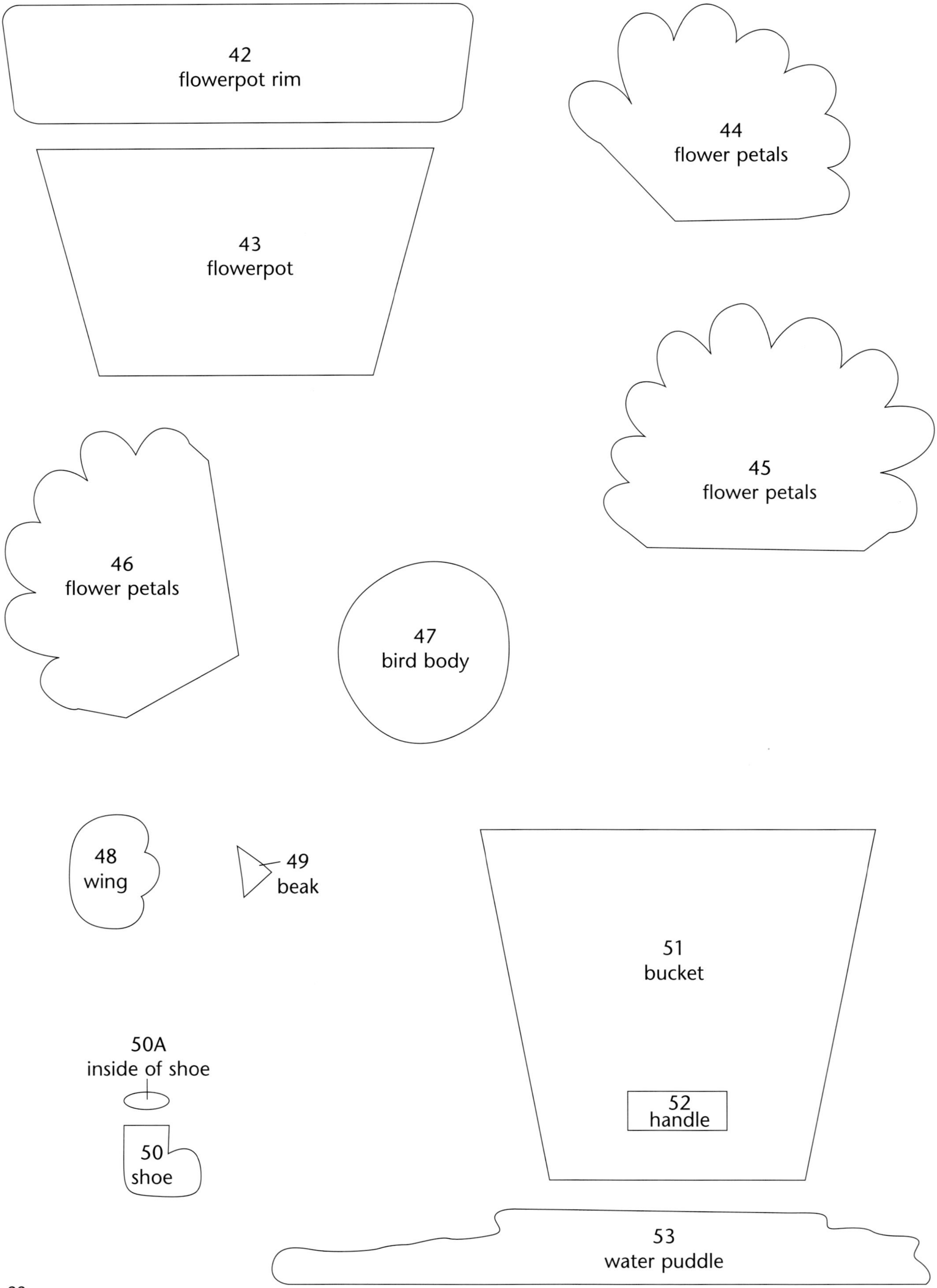
42
flowerpot rim
43
flowerpot
44
flower petals
45
flower petals
46
flower petals
47
bird body
48
wing
49
beak
50A
inside of shoe
50
shoe
51
bucket
52
handle
53
water puddle

54
flower petals
55
pocket
56
leaf
57
tulip petals
58
tulip
face
59
border flower
60
flower
center
61
border flower
62
flower center
63
border tulip
64
border
fence post

Workshop

Selecting Fabrics

The best fabric for quilts is 100% cotton. Yardage requirements in this book are based on 44"-wide fabric and allow for shrinkage. All fabrics, including backing, should be machine-washed, dried, and pressed before cutting. Use warm water and detergent but do not use fabric softener.

NECESSARY NOTIONS

- Scissors
- Rotary cutter and mat
- Acrylic rulers
- Template plastic
- Pencils for marking cutting lines
- Sewing needles
- Sewing thread
- Sewing machine
- Seam ripper
- Pins
- Iron and ironing board
- Quilting needles
- Thimble
- Hand-quilting thread
- Machine-quilting thread

Making Templates

A template is a duplication of a printed pattern; it is cut from a sturdy material and then used to trace the pattern onto fabric. Many regular shapes, such as squares and triangles, can be marked directly onto fabric with a ruler, but you need templates for other shapes. Some quiltmakers use templates for all shapes.

Trace patterns directly onto template plastic or make templates by tracing patterns onto graph paper and gluing the paper pieces to posterboard or sandpaper. (Sandpaper will not slip on fabric.) When a large pattern is given in two pieces, make one template for the complete piece.

Cut out the templates along the marked lines. Mark each template with its corresponding letter or number and the fabric's grain line. Verify the template's accuracy by placing it over the printed pattern. It is important that a template be traced, marked, and cut accurately. Any discrepancy, however small, is multiplied many times as the quilt is assembled. Another way to check the accuracy of templates is to make a test block before cutting more pieces.

Grain Lines

Woven threads form the fabric's grain. Lengthwise grain, parallel to the selvages, has the least stretch; crosswise grain has a little more give.

Long strips, such as borders, should be cut lengthwise whenever possible; also cut them first to ensure that you have the necessary length. Usually, you can cut other pieces aligned with either grain.

Bias is the 45° diagonal line between the two grain directions. Bias has the most stretch and is used for curved strips.

Never use the selvage (finished edge). Selvage does not react to washing, drying, and pressing like the rest of the fabric and may pucker when the finished quilt is laundered.

Rotary Cutting

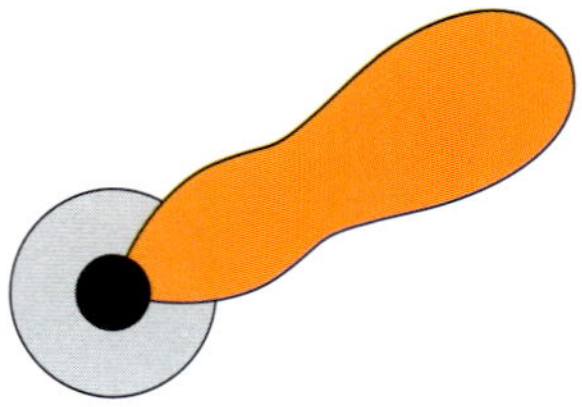

A rotary cutter, used with a protective mat and a ruler, takes getting used to but is very efficient for cutting strips, squares, and triangles. Using these tools makes quick work of cutting because you can measure and cut multiple layers with a single stroke, without making templates or marking pattern pieces. Using a rotary cutter is also more accurate than cutting with scissors because fabrics remain flat and do not move during cutting.

Because the blade is very sharp, be sure to get a rotary cutter with a safety guard. Keep the guard in the safe position at all times, except when making a cut. ***Always keep the cutter out of the reach of children.***

Use the cutter with a self-healing mat. A good mat for cutting strips is at least 23" wide. Here's how to use your rotary cutter.

1. Squaring the fabric is the first step in accurate cutting. Fold the fabric with the selvages aligned. With the yardage to your right, align a small square ruler with the fold near the cut edge. Place a long ruler against the left side of the square **(Diagram 1).** Keeping the longer ruler in place, remove the square. Hold the ruler in place with your left hand as you cut, rolling the cutter ***away from you*** along the ruler's edge with a steady motion. You can move your left hand along the ruler as you cut but do not change the position of the ruler. ***Keep your fingers away from the ruler's edge when cutting.***

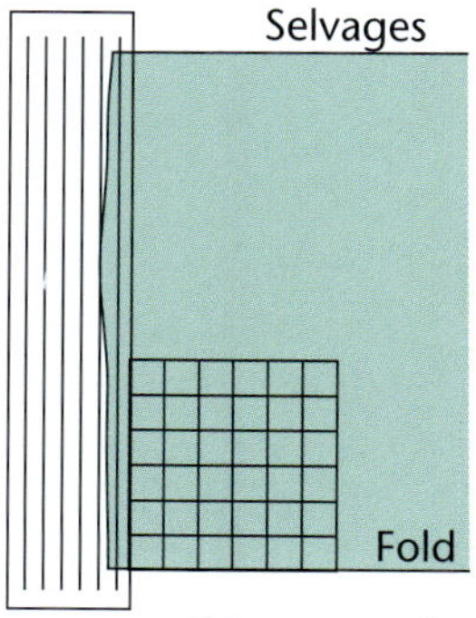

Diagram 1

2. Open the fabric. If the cut was not accurately cut perpendicular to the fold, the edge will be V-shaped instead of straight **(Diagram 2).**

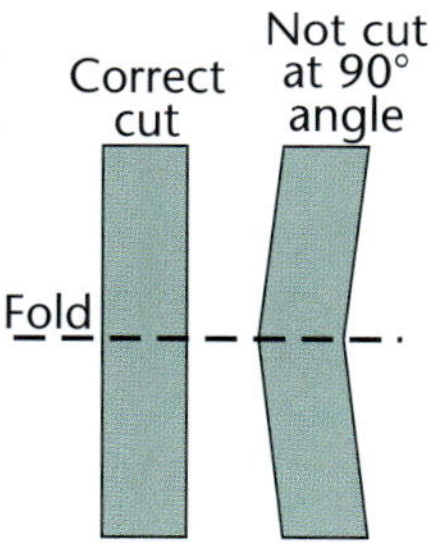

Diagram 2

3. With a transparent ruler, you can measure and cut at the same time. Fold the fabric in half again, aligning the selvages with the fold, making four layers that line up perfectly along the cut edge. Project instructions designate the strip width needed. Position the ruler to the desired measurement from the edge **(Diagram 3)** and cut. The blade will easily cut through all four of the layers. Check each strip to be sure the cut is straight. Each strip length is the width of the fabric, approximately 43" to 44". Using the ruler again, trim the selvages, cutting about ³⁄₈" from each end.

Diagram 3

4. To cut squares and rectangles from a strip, align the desired measurement on the ruler with the strip end and cut across the strip **(Diagram 4).**

Diagram 4

5. Cut triangles from squares or rectangles. Cutting instructions often direct you to cut a square in half or in quarters diagonally to make right triangles, and this technique can apply to rectangles, too **(Diagram 5).** The outside edges of the square or rectangle are on the straight of the grain, so triangle sides cut on the diagonal are bias.

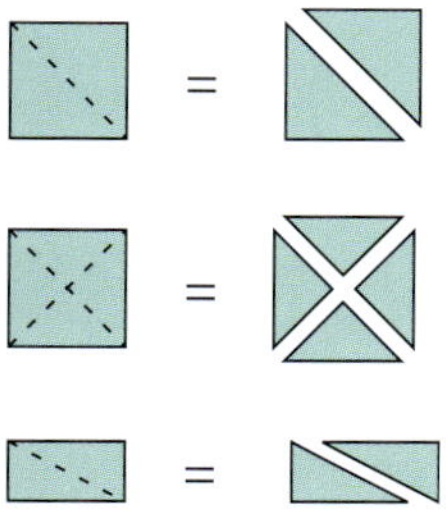
Diagram 5

What Is Fusible Appliqué?

Traditional appliqué is the process of sewing fabric shapes onto a background fabric, creating a layered design. Paper-backed fusible web simplifies this process by replacing the needle and thread. Paper-backed fusible web is a heat-activated adhesive with a temporary paper lining. A hot iron melts the glue, fusing fabric shapes to the base fabric. With this product, you can fuse any shape in place without sewing a stitch.

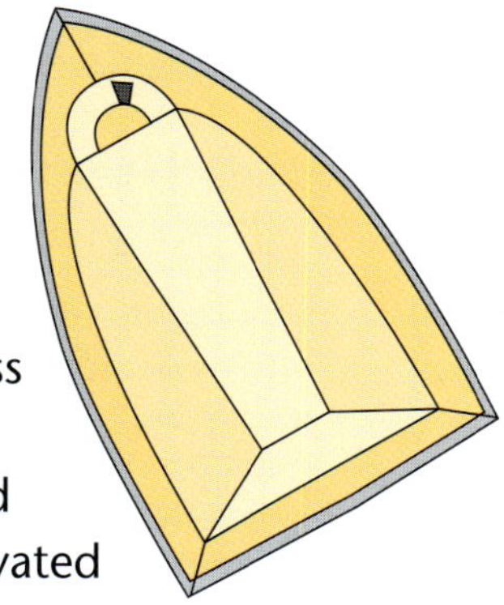

In traditional appliqué, turning under fabric edges can be challenging and time-consuming, especially on points, curves, and complex shapes. Fusible web eliminates this tedious chore: turning the edge isn't necessary because the web prevents raveling as it holds fabrics in place.

Fusible Facts

- Always prewash fabrics to remove sizing, which prevents fusible web from bonding with fabric.
- Use a damp press cloth, unless otherwise indicated. The press cloth protects your iron and provides moisture to fuse the web to the fabric. It also acts as a temperature and timing guide. After holding the iron on the press cloth for 10 to 15 seconds, the cloth should be dry. If it is still damp, more time or a higher temperature is needed.
- Keep in mind that the finished appliqué will be a mirror image of the pattern. So if a pattern points left, the appliqué will point right. **In this book, patterns are reversed as necessary.**
- Iron on a firm, padded surface. The padding helps absorb the moisture from the press cloth.
- Keep a supply of hot iron cleaner on hand. Available in most notions departments, the cleaner will remove any web adhesive that may stick to your iron.

Fusible Web How-tos

1. Trace the pattern onto the paper (smooth) side of the fusible web. Leaving a margin, roughly cut around the shape.
2. Place the web side of the fusible web onto the wrong side of the fabric. Press for five seconds with a hot, dry iron. Let the fabric cool. Cut out the shape along the pattern lines.
3. Remove the paper back from the fusible web.
4. Position the fabric appliqué, web side down, on your background block. (Fusible items can be held temporarily in place by "touch basting." Touch the item to be fused with the tip of the iron only. If the item is not in the desired position, it can be lifted and repositioned.)
5. To fuse, cover the fabric with a damp press cloth. Using an iron heated to the wool setting, press firmly for 10 seconds. Repeat, lifting and overlapping the iron until all the fabric is fused.
6. Remove the press cloth and iron the fabric to eliminate excess moisture.

TIPS AND TIDBITS

- The photos of each block are printed full size, so you can trace any embellishment details and then transfer them to your project.
- To make the ribbon embellishment for Jump Rope Jenny on page 8, tie the 8" length of red satin ribbon in a small bow at some point along the length. Using the photo as a placement guide, twist the ribbon slightly and drape it beneath the flower child. Attach the ends under the bumblebees. At several points along the ribbon, fasten by sewing on small heart buttons.
- Use fabric markers to draw details on the project pieces *before* you fuse them. That way, if you make a mistake or want to redo a facial feature, you can simply cut another piece without having to fuse over the incorrect piece.
- To give the flower children rosy cheeks, thin pink fabric paint with water. After you draw the face on the flower center, use a cotton swab to apply the fabric paint to the cheeks.
- If you tie buttons and charms onto the quilt using embroidery floss or twine, apply a drop of seam sealant to the knots or the centers of bows to secure them.
- Cut the bumblebee bodies from a yellow print fabric and then add stingers and stripes, using a permanent black fabric marker.
- This quilt's designer, Carol Burger, used a very thin polyester batting and tied the quilt at the corners of each block.

Fusible Appliqué Embellishment Techniques

- Fine-tipped fabric markers easily add details to appliqués. After cutting out an appliqué, place it over the pattern to trace details directly onto the fabric. To make a pattern easier to see, use a light box or tape the pattern to a bright windowpane. You can also use fine-tip markers to draw "quilting lines" around the edges of an appliqué, a technique called pen stitching.
- Buttons, beads, and charms create dimension. When sewn or glued in place, they can represent flowers, fashion accessories, and other details.
- Hand-embroidery stitches, such as running stitches or buttonhole stitches, add color, texture, and character to your work.

Measuring Borders

Because seams may vary and fabrics may stretch a bit, opposite sides of your assembled quilt top may not be the same measurement. You can (and should) correct this when you add borders.

Measure the length of each side of the quilt. Trim the side border strips to match the shorter of the two sides. Join borders to the quilt as described below, easing the longer side of the quilt to fit the border. Join borders to the top and bottom edges in the same manner.

Straight Borders

Side borders are usually added first **(Diagram 6).** With the right sides facing and the raw edges aligned, pin the center of one border strip to the center of one side of the quilt top. Pin the border to the quilt at each end and then pin along the side as desired. Machine-stitch with the border strip on top. Press the seam allowance toward the border. Trim excess border fabric at each end. In the same manner, add the border to the opposite side and then to the top and the bottom **(Diagram 7).**

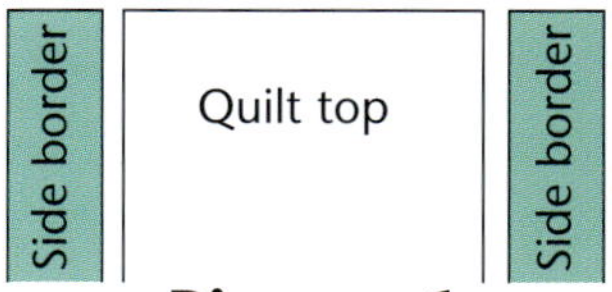

Diagram 6

Diagram 7

Mitered Borders

1. Measure your quilt sides. Trim the side border strips to fit the shorter side plus the width of the border ***plus*** 2".

2. Place a pin on the center of the quilt side and another pin at the center of the border.

3. With the right sides facing and the raw edges aligned, match the pins on the border strip to the center of the quilt. Working from the center out, pin the border to the quilt. (The border fabric will extend beyond the corners.)

4. Start machine-stitching at the top pin, backstitching to lock the stitches. Continue to sew, easing the fabric between the pins. Stop at the last pin; backstitch. Join the remaining borders in the same manner. Press the seam allowances toward the borders.

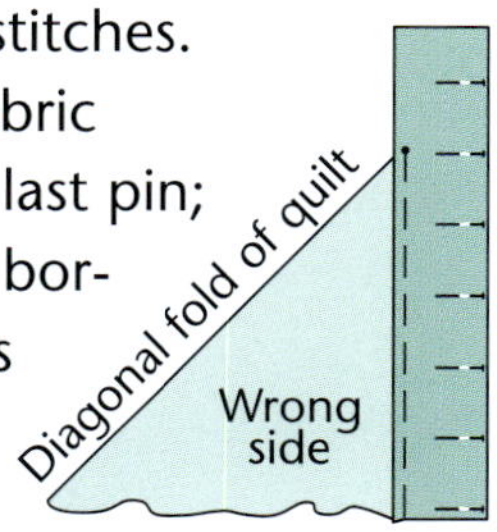

Diagram 8

5. With the right sides facing, fold the quilt diagonally, aligning the raw edges of the adjacent borders. Pin securely **(Diagram 8).**

6. Align a yardstick or a quilter's ruler along the diagonal fold **(Diagram 9).** Holding the ruler firmly, mark a line from the end of the border seam to the raw edge.

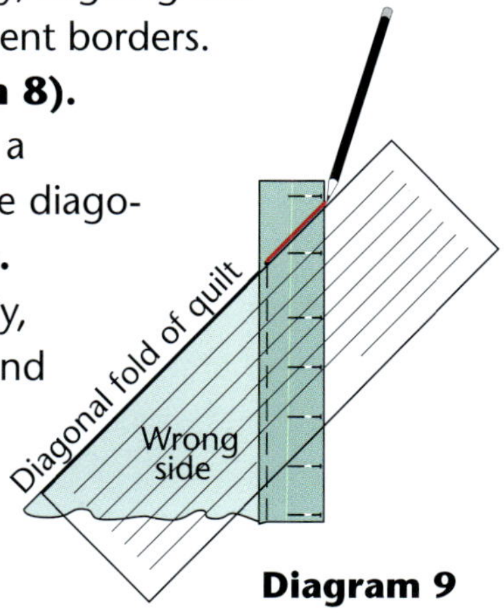

Diagram 9

7. Start machine-stitching at the beginning of the marked line, backstitch, and then stitch on the line out to the raw edge.

8. Unfold the quilt to be sure that the corner lies flat. Correct the stitching if necessary. Trim the seam allowance to ¼".

9. Miter the remaining corners in the same manner. Press the corner seams open.

Tying a Quilt

Instead of quilting, Carol Burger secured the layers of this quilt by tying. Tying is the fastest way to secure the three quilt layers and the only way to work with the thick batting often used for comforters. Colorful ties can also add a decorative effect to the overall design of your project.

Ties can be of pearl cotton, yarn, ribbon floss, or narrow ribbon. The material used for ties should be strong enough to be tied very tightly and stay tied. Ties may be double knots, bows, pom-poms, or knots that hold buttons, charms, or beads. ***Never use buttons or other small objects on quilts intended for babies or small children.***

You will need a sharp embroidery needle with an eye large enough to accommodate the tie material that you have chosen. Thread the needle but do not knot the thread end. Starting in the center of your basted quilt top, take a ⅛" to ¼" stitch through all three layers. Clip the thread, leaving a tail of thread several inches long on each side of the stitch **(Diagram 10).**

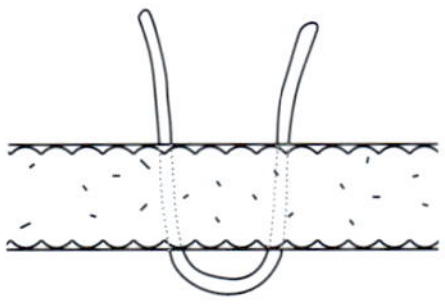

Diagram 10

Tie the two tails in a tight double knot **(Diagram 11).** Trim the tails of all the knots to the same length.

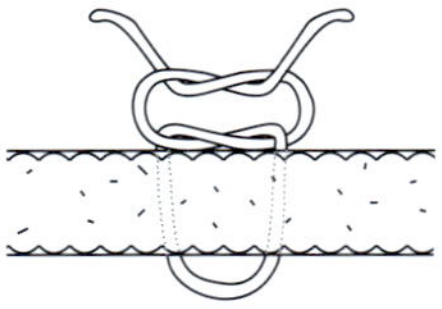

Diagram 11

If you want to tie a bow, leave longer tails and tie the double knot first; tie the tails in a bow. Then tie the loops of the bow in a knot to be sure that the knot is secure.

Quilting Without Marking

If you choose to quilt your project, consider stitching in-the-ditch (right along the seam line), outline-quilting (¼" from the seam line), or echo-quilting (lines of quilting rippling outward from the design like waves on a pond). These methods can be used without marking at all. If you are machine quilting, simply use the edge of your presser foot and the seam line as guides. If you are hand quilting, by the time you have pieced a quilt top, your eye will be practiced enough for you to produce straight, even quilting without the guidance of marked lines.

Marking Quilting Designs

If you choose quilting designs that need to be marked, here are some tips. The most common tool for this purpose is a sharp pencil. However, most pencils are made with an oil-based graphite lead, which often will not wash out completely. Look for a high-quality artist's pencil marked "2H" or higher (the higher the number, the harder the lead and the lighter the line it will make). Sharpen the pencil frequently to keep the line on the fabric thin and light. Or try a mechanical pencil with a 0.5-mm lead; it will maintain a fine line without sharpening.

While you are in the art-supply store, get a white plastic eraser (brand name Magic Rub). This eraser, used by professional drafters and artists, will cleanly remove the carbon smudges left by pencil lead without fraying the fabric or leaving eraser crumbs.

Water- and air-soluble marking pens are convenient—but controversial—marking tools. Some quilters have found that the marks reappear, often up to several years later, while others experience no problems with them.

Be sure to test these pens on each fabric you plan to mark and ***follow package directions precisely.*** Because the inks can be permanently set by heat, be very careful with a marked quilt. Do not leave it in your car on a hot day and never touch it with an iron until the marks have been removed. Plan to complete the quilting within a year after marking it with a water-soluble pen.

Air-soluble pens are best for marking small sections at a time. The marks disappear within 24 to 48 hours, but the ink remains in the fabric until it is washed. After the quilt is completed and before it is used, rinse it twice in clear, cool water, using no soap, detergent, or bleach. Let the quilt air-dry.

For dark fabrics, the cleanest marker you can use is a thin sliver of pure white soap. Choose a soap that contains no creams, deodorants, dyes, or perfumes; these added ingredients may leave a residue on the fabric.

Other marking tools include colored pencils made specifically for marking fabric and tailor's chalk (available in powdered, stick, and traditional cake form). When using chalk, mark small sections of the quilt at a time because the chalk rubs off easily.

Quilting Stencils

Quilting patterns can be purchased as precut stencils. Simply lay a stencil on your quilt top and mark the design through the cutout areas.

To make your own stencil of a printed quilting pattern, use a permanent marker to trace the design onto a blank sheet of template plastic. Then cut out the design with a craft knife.

Making a Quilt Backing

Some fabric and quilt shops sell 90" and 108" widths of 100%-cotton fabric that are very practical for quilt backing. However, the instructions in this book give backing yardages based on 44"-wide fabric.

When using 44"-wide fabric, all quilts wider than 41" will require a pieced backing. For quilts 41" to 80" wide, you will need an amount of fabric equal to two times the desired ***length*** of the unfinished backing. (The unfinished backing should be at least 3" larger on all sides than the quilt top.)

The simplest way to make a backing is to cut the fabric in half widthwise **(Diagram 12)** and

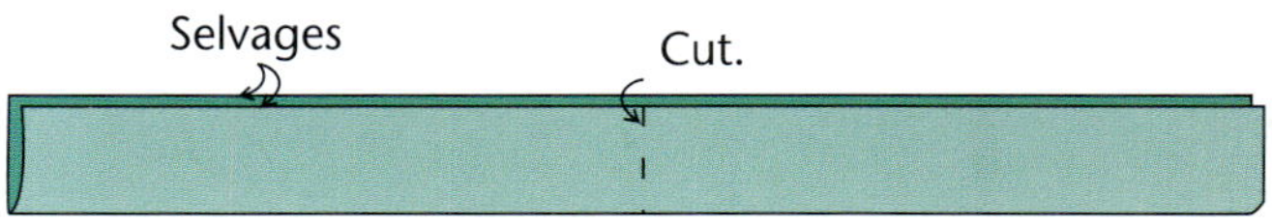

Diagram 12

then to sew the two panels together lengthwise. This results in a backing with a vertical center seam. Press the seam allowances to one side.

Another method of seaming the backing results in two vertical seams and a center panel of fabric. (This method is often preferred by quilt show judges.) Begin by cutting the fabric in half widthwise. Open the two lengths and stack them, with the right sides facing and the selvages aligned. Stitch along both selvage edges to create a tube of fabric **(Diagram 13).** Cut down the center of the top layer of fabric only and open the fabric flat **(Diagram 14).** Press the seam allowances to one side.

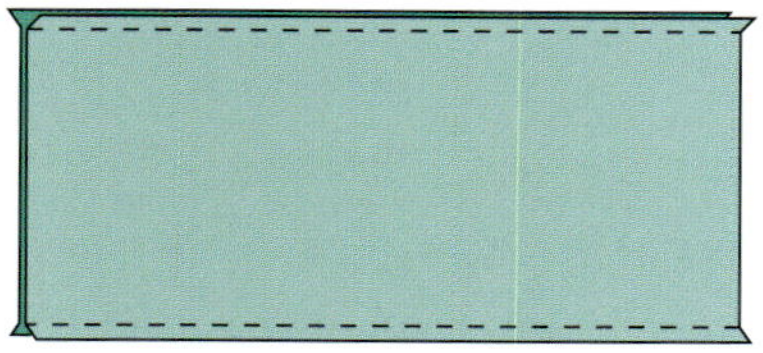

Diagram 13

Diagram 14

If the quilt is wider than 80", it is more economical to cut the fabric into three lengths that equal the desired width of the backing. Join the three lengths so that the seams are horizontal to the quilt, rather than vertical. For this method, you'll need an amount of fabric equal to three times the ***width*** of the unfinished backing.

Layering and Basting

After the quilt top and backing are made, the next steps are layering and basting to prepare for quilting or tying.

Prepare a large work surface to spread out the quilt—a large table, two tables pushed together, or the floor. Place the backing on the work surface, with the wrong side up. Unfold the batting and place it on top of the backing, smoothing away any wrinkles or lumps.

Lay the quilt top, with the right side up on top of the batting and the backing. Make sure the edges of the backing and the quilt top are parallel.

Basting keeps layers from shifting during quilting. Baste with a long needle and white thread (colored thread can leave a residue on light fabrics). Or use safety pins, if you prefer.

Start in the center and baste a line of stitches to each corner, making a large X. Then baste parallel lines 6" to 8" apart. Finish with a line of basting stitches ¼" from the edge.

Some quilters use nickel-plated safety pins for basting. Pin every 2" to 3". Don't close the pins as you go, as this can pucker the backing. When all pins are in place, gently tug the backing as you close each pin so that pleats don't form underneath.

Another popular method is to use a basting gun, which shoots plastic tabs through quilt layers. Use paper-cutting scissors to trim the tabs after the quilting is finished.

Hand Quilting

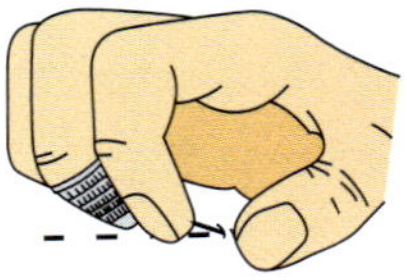

Hand-quilted stitches should be evenly spaced, with the spaces between the stitches about the same length as the stitches themselves. The ***number*** of stitches per inch is less important than the ***uniformity*** of the stitching. Don't worry if you take only five or six stitches per inch; just be consistent throughout the project.

Machine Quilting

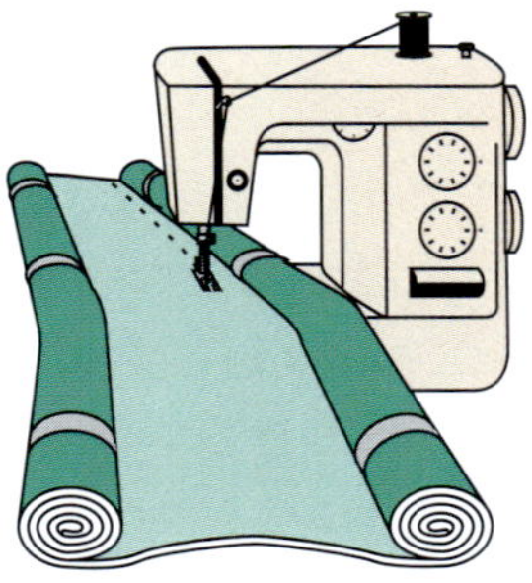

For machine quilting, the backing and the batting should be 3" larger all around than the quilt top, because the quilting process pushes the quilt top fabric outward. After quilting, trim the backing and the batting to the same size as the quilt top.

Thread your bobbin with good-quality sewing thread (not quilting thread) in a color to match the backing. Use a top thread color to match the quilt top or use invisible nylon thread.

An even-feed or walking foot will feed all the quilt's layers through the machine at the same speed. It is possible to machine-quilt without this foot (by experimenting with tension and presser foot pressure), but it will be much easier with it. If you do not have this foot, get one from your sewing machine dealer.

Continuous Straight-Grain Binding

1. Mark the fabric in horizontal lines equal to the width of the binding **(Diagram 15).**

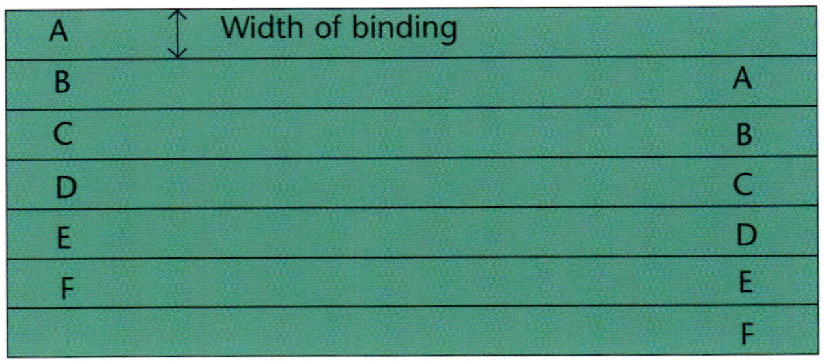

Diagram 15

2. With the right sides facing, fold the fabric in half, offsetting the drawn lines by matching the letters and the raw edges **(Diagram 16).** Stitch a ¼" seam.

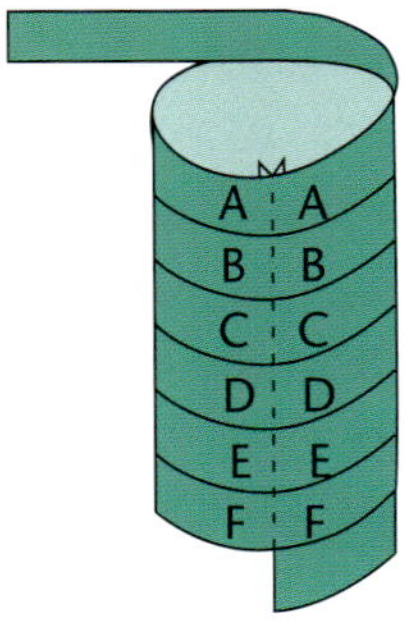

Diagram 16

3. Cut the binding in a continuous strip, starting with one end and following the marked lines around the tube. Press the strip in half lengthwise.

Continuous Bias Binding

This technique can be used to make continuous bias for appliqué as well as for binding.

1. Cut a square of fabric in half diagonally to form two triangles. With the right sides facing, join the triangles **(Diagram 17).** Press the seam allowance open.

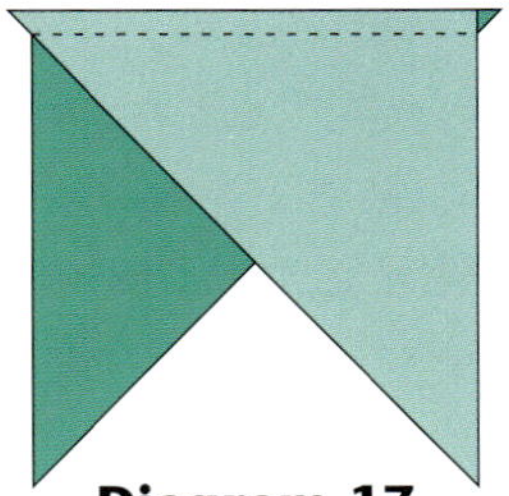

Diagram 17

2. Mark parallel lines equal to the desired

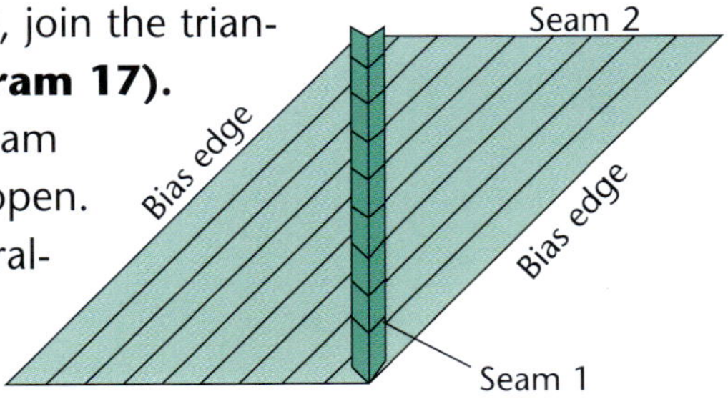

Diagram 18

width of the binding **(Diagram 18),** taking care not to stretch the bias. With the right sides facing, align the raw edges (indicated as Seam 2). As you align the edges, offset one Seam 2 point past its natural matching point by one line. Stitch the seam; then press the seam allowance open.

3. Cut the binding in a continuous strip, starting with the protruding point and following the marked lines around the tube **(Diagram 19).** Press the strip in half lengthwise.

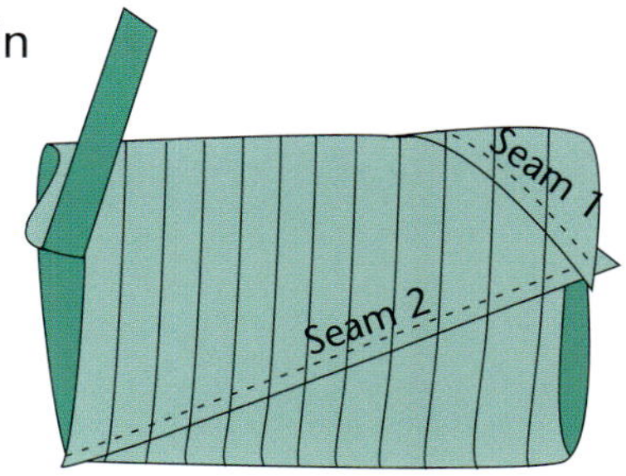

Diagram 19

Applying Binding

Binding is applied to the front of the quilt first. You may begin anywhere on the edge of the quilt except at the corner.

1. Matching raw edges, lay the binding on the quilt. Fold down the top corner of the binding at a 45° angle, align the raw edges, and pin **(Diagram 20).**

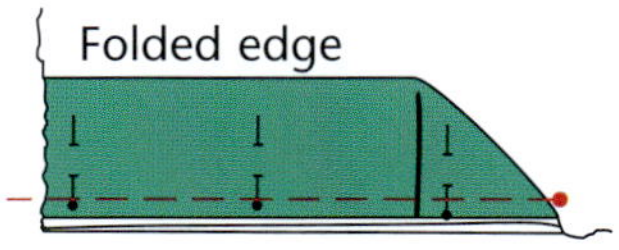

Diagram 20

2. Beginning at the folded end, machine-stitch the binding to the quilt. Stop stitching ¼" from the corner and backstitch. Fold the binding strip diagonally away from the quilt, making a 45° angle **(Diagram 21).**

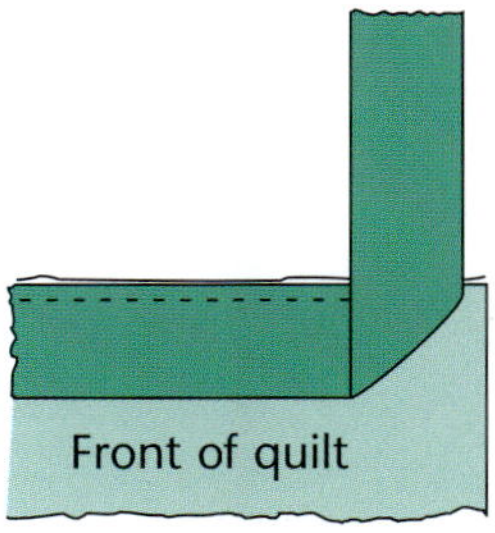

Diagram 21

3. Fold the binding strip straight down along the next side to be stitched, creating a pleat in the corner. Position the needle at the ¼" seam line of the new side **(Diagram 22).** Make a few stitches, backstitch, and then stitch the seam. Continue until all the corners and the sides are done. Overlap the end of the binding strip over the beginning fold and stitch about 2" beyond it. Trim any excess binding.

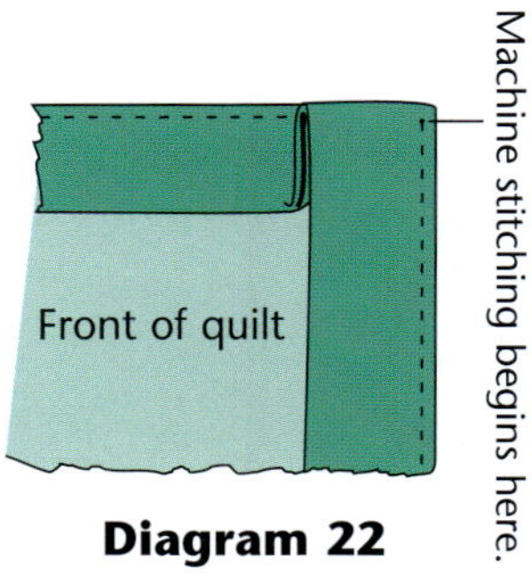

Diagram 22

4. Turn the binding over the raw edge of the quilt. Slipstitch it in place on the back, using thread that matches the binding. The fold at the beginning of the binding strip will create a neat, angled edge when it is folded to the back.

5. At each corner, fold the binding to form a miter **(Diagram 23).** Handstitch the miters closed if desired.

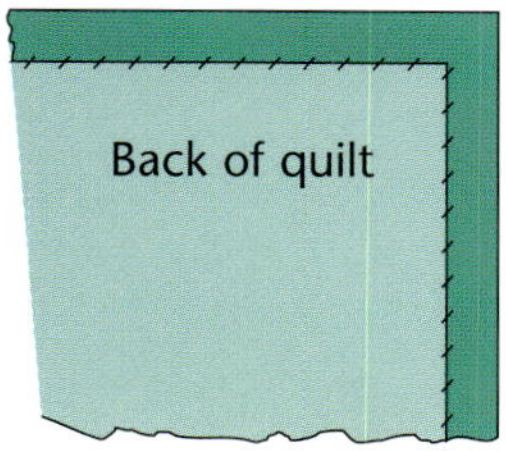

Diagram 23

Quilt Labels

Every quilt you make should include a quilt label. (See the example below.) You can appliqué or piece the label to the back or include the information in a quilt block on the front.

At a minimum, your quilt label should include:

- Name of the quilt
- Your name
- Your city and state
- Date of completion or date of presentation

Additional information can include the story behind the quilt, the maker, and/or the recipient. Consider recording how old you were when you made the quilt.

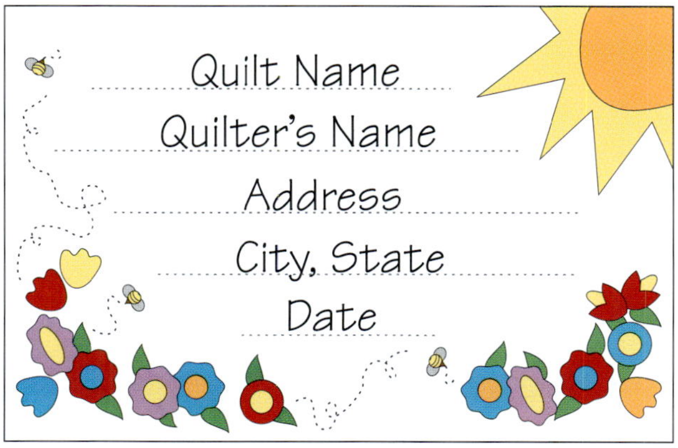

Sample Quilt Label Diagram

Quilt Labels

Trace, scan, or photocopy one of these quilt labels to finish your quilt.
Choose the top label for convenience or color the bottom label to match *your* quilt!